FANTASTIC BEASTS
AND WHERE TO FIND THEM™

POSTER BOOK

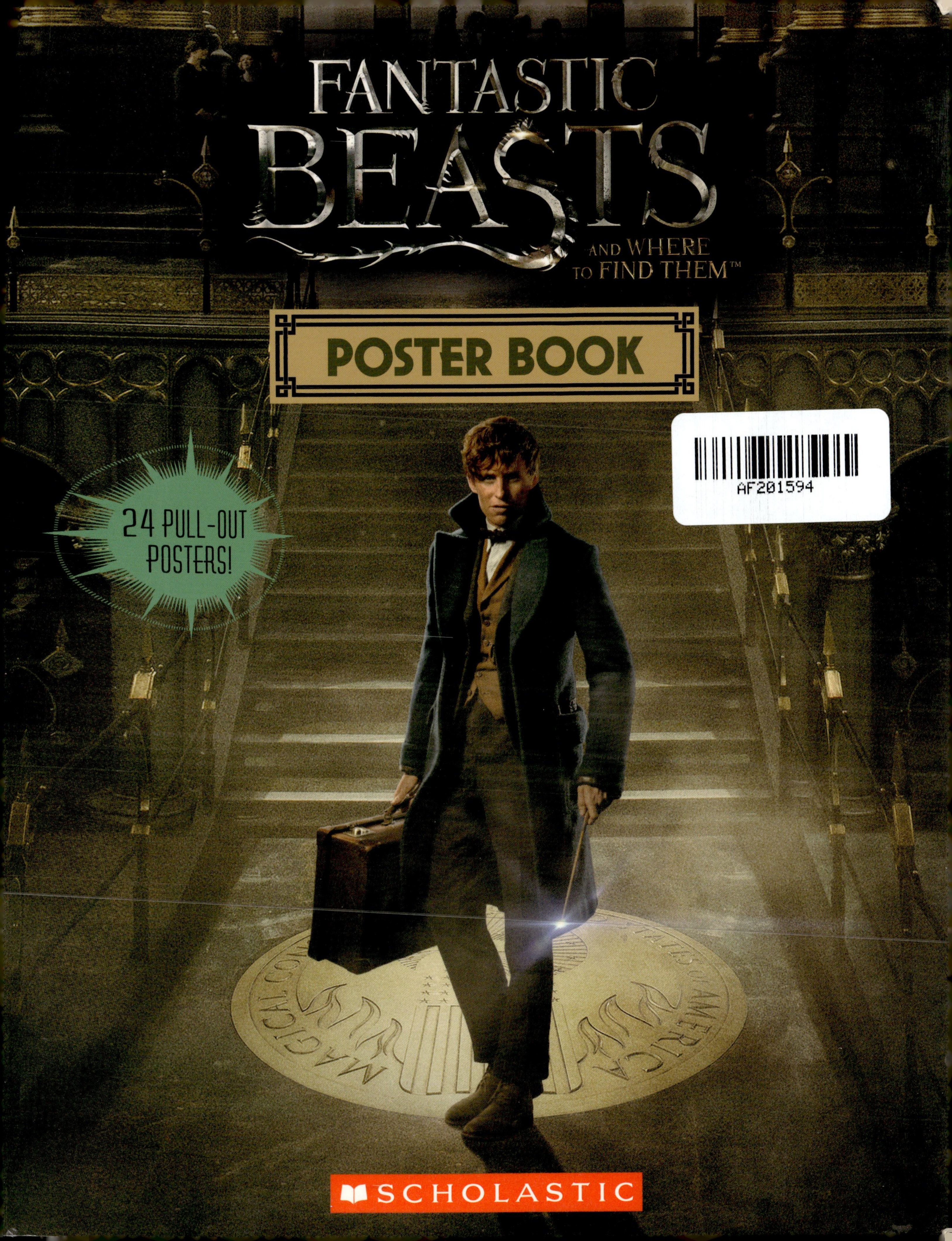

24 PULL-OUT POSTERS!

SCHOLASTIC

FANTASTIC BEASTS

AND WHERE

NEWT SCAMANDER
01
10
MAGIZOOLOGIST

FANTASTIC BEASTS AND WHERE TO FIND THEM
FIGHTING MODERN

A MAGICAL
WELCOME
TO
NEW YORK
FANTASTIC
BEASTS
TM & © WBEI

MUGGLE
WORTHY
FANTASTIC
BEASTS
AND WHERE TO FIND THEM

FANTASTIC
BEASTS
AND WHERE TO FIND THEM

FANTASTIC BEASTS AND WHERE TO FIND THEM

RESTAURA
& RENSO
PROVISIONS
FANTASTIC BEASTS AND WHERE TO FIND THEM

MAGICAL
CONGRESS
OF THE USA

No-Majs!

No-Magics

Non-Wizards

FANTASTIC
BEASTS
AND WHERE
TO FIND THEM
™ & © WBEI

NO-MAJ

FANTASTIC
BEASTS
AND WHERE TO FIND THEM
™ & © WBEI

FANTASTIC
BEASTS
AND WHERE
TO FIND THEM
™ & © WBEI

IT'S CHARMING!
NEW YORK
5 IMPERIAL
RESTAURANT
BEER IN TOWN
LIQUORS
FOR POSTAGE
FANTASTIC BEASTS AND WHERE TO FIND THEM
TM & © WBEI

FANTASTIC BEASTS AND WHERE TO FIND THEM

FANTASTIC
BEASTS
AND WHERE TO FIND THEM™

FANTASTIC BEASTS AND WHERE TO FIND THEM

FANTASTIC BEASTS AND WHERE TO FIND THEM
™ & © WBEI

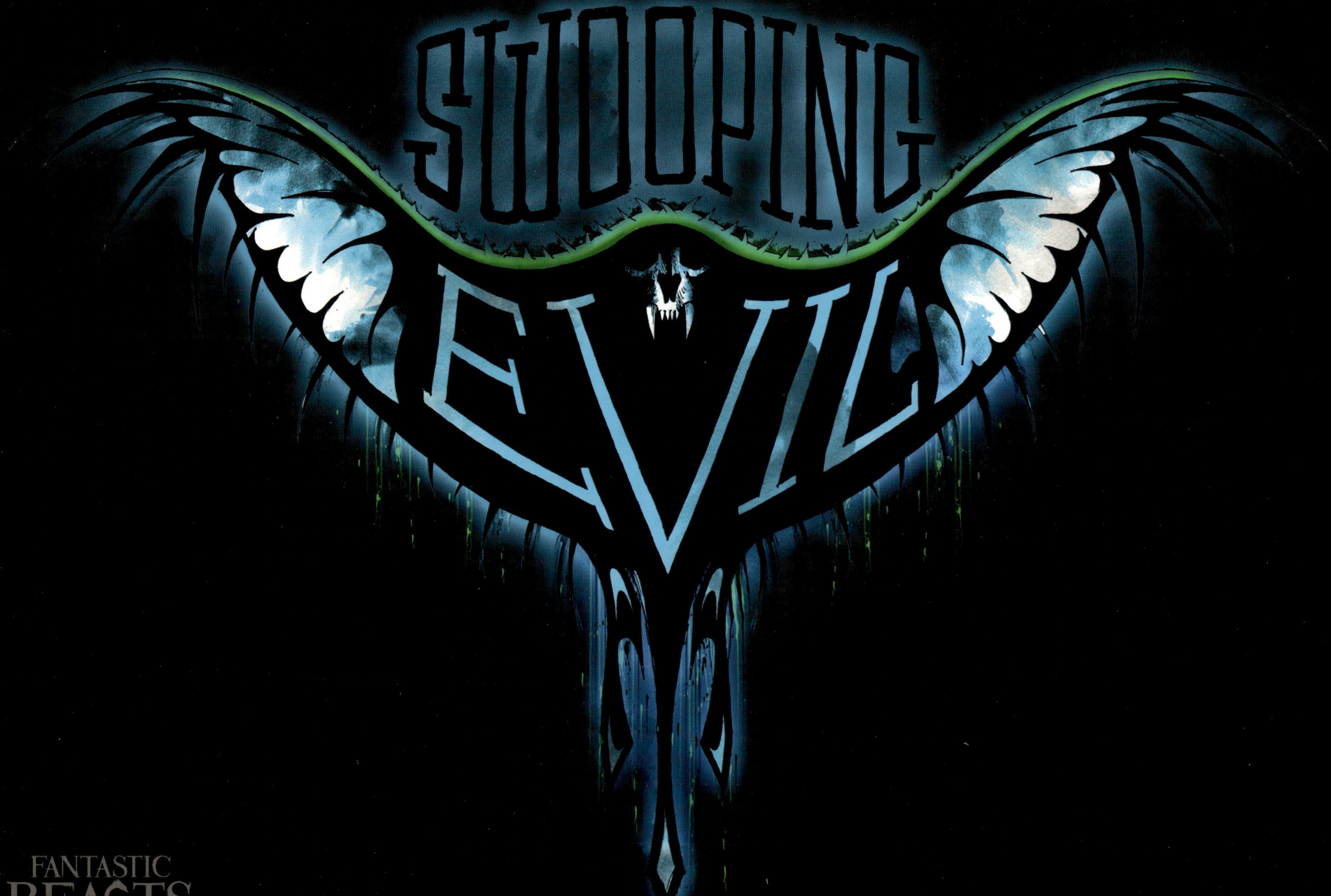

FANTASTIC BEASTS and WHERE to FIND THEM

ACCIO
FANTASTIC
BEASTS
TM & © WBEI

FANTASTIC BEASTS

FANTASTIC
BEASTS
AND WHERE
to FIND THEM
™ & © WBEI

Fly to New York for...
...a Broom with a View
New
London
FOR POSTAGE
FANTASTIC BEASTS
AND WHERE TO FIND THEM

BRING HOME THE MAGIC OF
FANTASTIC BEASTS AND WHERE TO FIND THEM™
WITH THESE 24 STUNNING IMAGES.

SCHOLASTIC

8187 SCHOLASTIC.COM

ISBN: 978-93-86106-55-1
Printed at Parksons Graphics, Mumbai (India)

First printing 2016
Art Director: Rick DeMonico

Reprinted by
Scholastic India Pvt. Ltd.
A-27, Ground Floor, Sigma Centre
Infocity-1, Sector 34,
Gurgaon 122001 (India)

FSC
www.fsc.org
MIX
Paper from responsible sources
FSC® C122244

Poster Book ₹350
ISBN 978-93-86106-55-
9 789386 106551
SCHOLASTIC
www.scholastic.co.in